Not by Bread Alone

Daily Reflections for Lent 2015

LITURGICAL PRESS

Collegeville, Minnesota

www.litpress.org

Nihil Obstat: Reverend Robert Harren, *Censor deputatus*

Imprimatur: ✠ Most Reverend Donald J. Kettler, J.C.L., Bishop of Saint Cloud, Minnesota, May 22, 2014.

Cover design by Ann Blattner. Photo courtesy of Thinkstock by Getty Images.

ISSN: 1550-803X

ISBN: 978-0-8146-3561-2   978-0-8146-3586-5 (ebook)

Introduction

We spend much of our lives in one desert or another; we travel through many wildernesses in the course of our days: terrifying, confusing, intimidating times and places when and where every move is a tentative step into the unknown.

We have all found ourselves in deserts of waiting, of emptiness, of indecision. We have all wandered through the wildernesses of rejection, of anger, of despair. In these stark and empty places, we look for some cairn of God's presence, some oasis of God's grace. Unemployment and the anxious search for a new job, a shattered relationship and the mending of a broken heart, the difficult ending of one phase of life and the unsure transition into a new—all deserts calling us to new decisions, all wildernesses through which we seek a new path home.

Every Lent the Spirit of God that drove Jesus into the desert drives us into the desert of our hearts, into the wilderness within us where God dwells. The desert of our hearts is the silent place where God speaks to us of hope and encouragement; it is the quiet wood where we clear our heads to realize what is right and good; it is the bright vista that opens our eyes to realize the path we should take if we are to become the people of justice and righteousness that we seek to become. In this Lenten springtime, the Spirit calls our souls into the desert in order to discern what God calls us to make of the time we have been given, to re-center our lives with new hope and renewed vision as we continue our journey to the Easter promise. Every important decision we make in our lives takes place in that desert with Jesus; every milestone, every first experience, begins in that wilderness with Christ.

These six weeks are a desert journey of the heart with Jesus: We follow him from his desert retreat to the Mount of the Transfiguration, from his teaching and preaching in the Galilean countryside to Jerusalem, from his Passover supper with his closest friends to the Passover of his body and spirit, from the cross of Good Friday to the empty tomb of Easter morning. The reflections in this year's edition of *Not by Bread Alone* are signposts for this Lent's desert retreat, markers of God's presence in the everyday wilderness experiences of death and resurrection.

May the pages that follow give you moments to stop and realize the love of God within your family, community, and church. May the stories, reflections, and prayers help you transform your deserts into the greenery of God's joy, and may they serve as a light to illuminate your way through life's tangled and terrifying wilderness.

Reflections

February 18: Ash Wednesday

The M&M's of Lenten Conversion

Readings: Joel 2:12-18; 2 Cor 5:20–6:2; Matt 6:1-6, 16-18

Scripture:
Rend your hearts, not your garments,
   and return to the LORD, your God. (Joel 2:13)

Reflection: Nine-year-old David decides to give up his favorite candy for Lent—M&M's. He's good for a bag a day, so forty bags (rounded out to one dollar a bag) comes to $40 over Lent. On top of that, Mom and Dad offer to match his Lenten sacrifice dollar for dollar.

So, on Easter Sunday, David's Lenten discipline results in net earnings of $80.

Now what to do with the money?

In school David learns about a nonprofit group that drills water wells in poor African countries. Done. David gives his $80 to the organization. He receives a letter of thanks, and David is now on their mailing list. Every few weeks, David receives a newsletter about new projects made possible by donations like his $80.

That $80 was earned several Lents ago. But David still supports the program and many others like it. The Lenten sacrifice of his childhood instilled in the now-adult David a deep, permanent sense of compassion and empathy.

David's Lenten sacrifice of M&M's is a model of Lenten conversion. Lent calls us to sacrifice and penance—but not out of self-loathing or false humility. Lent is the season to "turn" away (the word *conversion* means "to turn") from our own needs and wants in order to see a world larger than ourselves. David's "sacrifice" leads him to a new appreciation for what he has and opens his heart to the needs of others; his Lenten "turning" results in a lifelong "turning" to generosity and empathy.

May we take on that same kind of sacrifice this Lent. Over the next forty days, give up something—money, time, attitudes—that has the potential to yield a new perspective that will last well beyond this Easter Sunday.

Meditation: How can you make the next forty days a time of true conversion that lasts well beyond Easter?

Prayer: God of mercy and compassion, be with us on the journey to Easter that we begin today. Open our hearts to hear your call to holy sacrifice, that these days may be a time for healing and restoration leading to a permanent change of heart and transformation of our perspectives and attitudes. Help us to find within ourselves your grace so that we may transform our lives and our world from the ashes of division and selfishness to the peace and hope of Easter.

Resurrection Road

Readings: Deut 30:15-20; Luke 9:22-25

Scripture:
   "If anyone wishes to come after me, he must deny
      himself
and take up his cross daily and follow me.
For whoever wishes to save his life will lose it,
   but whoever loses his life for my sake will save it."
      (Luke 9:23-24)

Reflection: The great mathematician Euclid was engaged by the royal family to tutor the young heir to the throne. Patiently and precisely, Euclid explained to his young charge the basic theorems of geometry, but the prince was having a great deal of trouble grasping the principles.

Finally, the prince burst out in utter frustration, "Is there no simple way you can get to the point? Surely the crown prince need not be expected to concern himself with such minutiae."

Euclid quietly but firmly replied, "Alas, sire, there is no royal road to learning."

We tend to look at the gospel from our modern, sophisticated perspective and quietly dismiss what Jesus says as too unrealistic or simplistic to tackle our complex problems. We are interested in high-tech answers to our high-tech problems;

we cannot be bothered with such unrealistic "minutiae" like love for one another, forgiveness, compassion, justice.

But, to paraphrase Euclid, there is no "royal" road to God; there is no modern, high-tech approach to the gospel values of justice and mercy; there is no comfortable, easy alternative to taking up our own crosses as Jesus takes up his and walking the road Jesus walks to the kingdom of God.

The path to God begins outside of ourselves; the Easter promise is fulfilled by the hard way of the cross.

Meditation: What do you struggle to "deny" yourself in order to more fully live the Gospel of Jesus?

Prayer: Christ Jesus, give us the courage and conviction to take up the crosses laid upon our shoulders. Help us to "crucify" our own narrow interests and self-centered wishes so that we may bring to our families and communities the joy and hope of Easter.

The Spirit of Lenten Fasting

Readings: Isa 58:1-9a; Matt 9:14-15

Scripture:
"Can the wedding guests mourn
    as long as the bridegroom is with them?" (Matt 9:15)

Reflection: Rabbi Joseph Telushkin, in *The Book of Jewish Values*, offers this different take on fasting as a prayer:

"My wife and I . . . periodically try to engage in a 'complaining fast.' For a week at a time, we try to refrain from all whining and complaining. What generally motivates us to initiate such a fast is a spate of constant grumbling. It frequently happens that one of us will start complaining about what a hard week or month we have been having. More often than not, such complaints at first evoke sympathy, but soon prompt the other spouse to start recalling every difficulty he or she has been having that week or month. Often, such conversations quickly escalate into a delineation of all the difficulties we are experiencing. By the time the discussion is finished, we are aware of everything in our lives that is not going well, and we are both miserable. . . .

"One way to achieve more happiness is to declare a temporary moratorium on complaining. Doing so makes it easier to become conscious of things that are going well in your life."

Especially during Lent, we usually identify fasting with giving up something tangible like food and drink. But the hunger we feel in our stomachs reminds us of our more important hunger for the things of God. This Lent perhaps we might consciously fast from other intangibles, like how we respond and behave:

- fasting from complaining, as Rabbi Telushkin suggests, so as to become more aware of all that we have to be grateful for in our lives;
- fasting from criticism, so as to see anew the good that exists in everyone;
- fasting from anger, so as to realize our own need for forgiveness and understanding.

We might also consider a fast from television in order to spend more time with our families; a fast from "me time" in order to volunteer our time to some charity; a fast from "noise" in order to spend time in silent, conscious, attentive prayer.

The spirit of fasting is not what we fast *from*, but what fasting enables us to *do*, how fasting enables us to shift our focus and attention from the ordinary to the things of God.

Meditation: What might you "fast" from this Lent that would free you to do something meaningful and enriching?

Prayer: Christ, bridegroom of the Father's wedding feast, may our fasting this Lent bring us to a new awareness of your loving presence in our lives and satisfy our hunger for the joy and grace that comes from you alone. By your grace, help us this Lent to put aside the things that separate us from you and bring the joy and hope of your resurrection into our homes and hearts.

Good Spring Soil

Readings: Isa 58:9b-14; Luke 5:27-32

Scripture:
Jesus saw a tax collector named Levi sitting at the customs
post.
He said to him, "Follow me." (Luke 5:27)

Reflection: Farmers and gardeners will all tell you—humus
is gold in their fields and gardens.

Composed of the decay of plant and animal matter, humus
is the most organic and richest part of the soil. When it is
tilled and broken open to receive seed and rainfall and sun-
light to nurture the seed, the dark humus yields the most
bountiful harvests and the most beautiful of flowers.

From the same root as "humus" comes the English word
humility. Like the rich, broken soil of humus, humility is the
capacity to be open to receive the seeds of experience—both
the painful and the enriching—in order to grow in wisdom
and understanding. Humility is the grace to let ourselves be
"broken"—broken of our pride, our ego, our wants—in order
to realize a harvest far greater than ourselves, a harvest that
is possible only through generous openness, selfless giving,
and enlightened gratitude. Humility is the grace to plant in
hope, to persevere through droughts and storms, to reap in
joy.

Humility is not denigrating ourselves but respecting others, realizing that, regardless of our own talents and gifts, we stand with every human being as brothers and sisters before God. Humility recognizes and honors the gifts of everyone, gifts as valuable as our own and deserving to be of service to the common good.

Authentic faith is centered in such humility: humility that begins with valuing life as a gift from God, a gift we have received only through God's mysterious love, not through anything we have done to deserve it. In faith that begins with such spiritual "humus," we can bring forth love from barrenness, we can find reason to hope in the midst of despair, and we can see the light that enables us to make our way out of the darkest places.

The Risen One promises us that the seeds of joy, trust and community that we plant even in the hardest soil and nurture in the coldest winters will take root and blossom and yield a miraculous harvest.

Meditation: What hard soil in your life needs to be broken in order for a new sense of purpose and joy to spring up?

Prayer: Gracious God, Giver of all life, plant the seed of your Word within us. During this Lenten season, may that Word take root in the "humus" of our hearts, that we may realize the harvest of your joy and mercy in every season of the year.

When Life Begins

Readings: Genesis 9:8-15; 1 Peter 3:18-22; Mark 1:12-15

Scripture:
The Spirit drove Jesus out into the desert,
    and he remained in the desert for forty days,
        tempted by Satan. (Mark 1:12-13)

Reflection: You are in the midst of a job search.
    You are fighting your insurance company to cover a
        catastrophic loss or medical care for a family member.
    You are working through therapy to overcome an illness
        or disability.
    You are juggling several courses to finish your degree.
    You are buried in a critical project at work.
    Things you want to do, dreams you want to realize, are
        put on hold.
    You find yourself saying, *I can't wait for my life to begin . . .*
    And you imagine: *My life will begin when . . .*
    My life will begin when I finish school.
    My life will begin when I get a new job.
    My life will begin when I know my children will be fine.
    *My life will begin when the tuitions are covered and our
        retirement is funded.*
    My life will begin when I finish . . .

Today, Jesus confronts the "beginning" of his own life. In his confrontation with Satan, Jesus comes to understand exactly what the Father is calling him to do. We find ourselves confronting the same question: how to live our "imperfect" lives to the fullest, to the happiest, to the most meaningful.

Lent calls us to realize that our lives begin *now*.

This Lenten spring is a time for finding our way out of our winters of cynicism, our deserts of self-absorption, our wildernesses of despair and hopelessness. These days before Easter's dawning are a time for deciding what we want our lives to be, what values we want to make the center of our lives, what we believe to be truly meaningful and purposeful to us.

For our lives begin now; heaven is before us.

Meditation: How can you make this Lenten season a new beginning?

Prayer: O God, lead us this Lent into the deserts of our hearts. Let these days be a time of discernment and discovery, of resolution and conversion, that this springtime may be a season for beginnings and new growth in our lives. May your Word be our bread during our wilderness journey; may your light illuminate the treacherous turns of the road we walk; may your grace and wisdom minister to us in our deserts of sadness and despair.

Christ at the Monastery Door

Readings: Lev 19:1-2, 11-18; Matt 25:31-46

Scripture:
"'Amen, I say to you, whatever you did
for one of these the least brothers of mine, you did for
me.'" (Matt 25:40)

Reflection: In the Nikos Kazantzakis novel *The Greek Passion*, the story is told of an old monk who dreamed of travelling to Jerusalem to pray at the Holy Sepulcher. Over the years, the monk managed to put aside what money he could. Finally, near the end of his life, he had enough to embark on his pilgrimage.

But no sooner had he left the monastery when he encountered a man in rags, bent to the ground, picking herbs and wild berries.

"Where are you going, Father?" the man asked.

The old monk explained that he was going off to Jerusalem, to the Church of the Holy Sepulcher, to realize his dream to "go thrice around the Holy Sepulcher and bow down" in prayer before God.

"How much money do you have, Father?" inquired the man.

"Thirty pounds," the monk answered.

"Give me the thirty pounds, I've a wife and children and they're hungry. Give them to me, go thrice around me, fall on your knees and bow down before me; then afterward go back into your monastery."

Filled with compassion, the monk took the thirty pounds from his travel bag and gave it all to the poor man. The monk walked three times around him, knelt, and went back through the gates of his monastery.

The old monk returned to his cloister, forever changed—for he realized that the beggar was Christ himself. He had encountered Christ not in some holy place far away, but right outside his monastery door.

The monk was blessed with the vision of humanity that Jesus articulates in the parable of the sheep and the goats: a vision that realizes the holiness of God within every man, woman and child; a vision of humanity that sees deeper than the externals of race, nationality, culture and language to behold the life of God animating the lives of all who draw breath; a vision that, once realized, changes not only those we are able to assist but changes us, as well.

Meditation: Have you encountered Christ in the humility, the generosity, or the poverty of someone you have met?

Prayer: Compassionate God, open our eyes to see you in the faces of the poor, the troubled, and the forgotten; open our hands to reach out to them in your hope and peace. May we give you thanks for your many blessings to us by seeking to share those blessings with all our brothers and sisters in Christ Jesus.

February 24: Tuesday of the First Week of Lent

Prayer of the Water Bowl

Readings: Isa 55:10-11; Matt 6:7-15

Scripture:
"This is how you are to pray:
Our Father who art in heaven . . .
thy will be done,
    on earth as it is in heaven." (Matt 6:9, 10)

Reflection: In her book *My Grandfather's Blessings*, Rachel Naomi Remen writes about a ritual taught to her by an elderly Tibetan nun.

In the morning, immediately after rising, she takes a bowl and fills it with water. As she fills the bowl, she reflects on the particulars of her life: the people she cares about, the problems she is facing, the success and disappointments she is experiencing. As the bowl fills with water, Dr. Remen writes, "you receive your life openheartedly and unconditionally as your portion. Walking very slowly so as not to spill a drop out of the brimming bowl, you take it to a private place in your home . . . dedicating all that it contains to the service of life."

There the bowl of water sits until the end of the day. The last thing Dr. Remen does before going to sleep is take the bowl outside and empty the water into the earth and then return the bowl to its place, upside down. For Dr. Remen, "this cycle of openheartedly taking on whatever one has been given, using it all to serve the life around you, then letting it go completely refers as much to the wisdom of a lifetime as it does to the wisdom of living each day."

The gift of faith enables us to see the world and everything and everyone in it as a gift from the God whose love for us knows neither beginning nor end. That is prayer: to realize, with humility and gratitude, that God fills the simple "bowls" of our lives with the "water" of his life and love.

In today's Gospel, Jesus gives us much more than the words to the prayer that has come down to us as "The Lord's Prayer"—Jesus instills in us the attitude in which all prayer should be centered: recognizing God as the loving Father of us all, seeking God's way of mercy and justice in all things, being aware and grateful for God's countless blessings to us, and seeking forgiveness by forgiving others.

Meditation: What daily ritual or prayer could you practice that would help you develop a prayerful perspective of gratitude and openheartedness?

Prayer: Father in heaven, do not let us confine our prayer to words and rituals alone. Open our hearts and inspire our spirits to work and sacrifice for the hopes and dreams we ask of you. May every moment you give us be part of a continuous lifelong prayer of praise to you, you who are the Giver and Sustainer of all life.

The Queen of the South

Readings: Jonah 3:1-10; Luke 11:29-32

Scripture:
"At the judgment
   the queen of the south will rise with the men of this
      generation
   and she will condemn them,
   because she came from the ends of the earth
   to hear the wisdom of Solomon,
   and there is something greater than Solomon here."
   (Luke 11:31)

Reflection: In today's Gospel, Jesus makes two references to
Old Testament figures.

One is the prophet Jonah, who reluctantly went to preach
to the dissolute city of Nineveh. Despite his frustration and
doubt about his mission, Jonah came to trust enough in God
and his Word to carry out his seemingly futile mission.

But the second Old Testament reference is one we may not
have heard before: "the queen of the south." It is a story
recounted in the First Book of Kings about David's son and
successor, Solomon. Because of his wisdom, devotion, and
wealth, Solomon was held in profound respect not only by
his own people but by the rulers of surrounding kingdoms.
The queen of Sheba (most likely present-day Yemen) had

heard about the wise and skilled king of Israel and decided to come and meet him and see his kingdom for herself.

The queen and her retinue received a gracious welcome from Solomon. She was deeply impressed by Solomon's wisdom and insight and the peace and prosperity enjoyed by his people—but most of all, she understood that it was all grounded in Solomon and Israel's trust and faith in their God.

Jesus holds up the penitents of Nineveh and the queen "of the south" as models of true seekers of God, who possess the openness of spirit and integrity of heart to welcome God's justice and peace in their midst, who are willing to endure great hardship and sacrifice to travel great distances—literally and figuratively—to find God. Now Jesus admonishes his hearers that an even greater sign of God's love than Jonah and Solomon is among them now, but they are too obtuse in their self-absorption and fear to realize it.

God's risen Christ is in our midst in every experience of love and forgiveness that blesses our place and time.

Meditation: How is your life a "sign" of God's love among your family and community?

Prayer: Open our eyes and humble our spirits, Lord God, to see the signs of your love, justice, and forgiveness in our midst. May we, in turn, become effective signs of your compassionate presence in this time and place of ours, signs of your call to reconciliation, signs of your spirit of justice and mercy in the Ninevehs of our homes, schools, and workplaces.

"A Hole in the Bottom of the Basket"

Readings: Esth C:12, 14-16, 23-25; Matt 7:7-12

Scripture:
"If you, then, who are wicked,
   know how to give good things to your children,
   how much more will your heavenly Father give good
      things
   to those who ask him." (Matt 7:11)

Reflection: A pastor was asked if his parish could help some children in a nearby town who needed new clothes for school. He discussed it with the staff and pastoral council, and they decided to donate a percentage of the profits from the parish's annual fundraiser. The event turned out to be the parish's most successful ever.

So the parish decided to continue to make charity a part of other parish fundraising projects—and the results were even better. A spirit of generosity began to build in the parish. People now regularly send in checks to be "given to someone in need." The parish staff has been able to quietly help with mortgage payments, tuition costs, and house repairs. Even though the privacy of those assisted is strictly protected, word of such help is getting out and more and more parishioners want to help.

And none of this has lessened the Sunday collection—in fact, the pastor writes, the Sunday offering "has increased every year, along with Mass attendance and parish enrollment. I suppose it all has to do with trust. Even with fewer dollars at their disposal, people want to participate in good works. We all have to trust that God is continually at work, figuring things out, planting ideas, making connections, and passing the basket. Or, in other words, a good way to increase the Sunday collection is to put a hole in the basket."

Today's Gospel is about such trust—trust in God's vision of a world united in his love and trust in our ability to realize that vision in our own Christ-like works of compassion and reconciliation. Such a sense of trust, Jesus teaches, begins in our approach to prayer. In many of our prayers, we ask God to come around to doing our will; but true prayer is to discover God's will for us. Prayer worthy of God seeks the grace to do the work God calls us to do (forgiveness, charity, justice) and to become the people God calls us to become (brothers and sisters under the one heavenly Father).

Meditation: When has your trust in God, however tentative, been rewarded in ways you never expected?

Prayer: Good and gracious God, guide our hearts, that we may see you in one another and walk in your light as we travel through this lifetime. Take our hands in yours and set them to the work of making our prayers for love, reconciliation, and justice realities in our time and place.

Wins and Losses

Readings: Ezek 18:21-28; Matt 5:20-26

Scripture:
"You have heard that it was said to your ancestors,
You shall not kill; and whoever kills is liable to judgment.
But I say to you, whoever is angry with his brother
will be liable to judgment. (Matt 5:21-22)

Reflection: You're in the right, everyone says. It's their fault, not yours. The law is on your side, you have been assured. Take advantage of the situation, they urge—you should be compensated for your injury and inconvenience. Besides, the insurance company will be footing the bill, so don't worry. But it's not that simple; the whole thing makes you uneasy.

They acted horribly—as they always do. And every time they come, there's a scene. So this time you didn't include them. The tension level dropped dramatically, and everyone had a much better time as a result. But the anger and hurt is still there, even if they are not.

The course is required for graduation. But you're learning nothing: the professor's lectures are obtuse, the readings dense. It's an exercise in futility. But you need these credits, so you manage to get by with a C and move on. But what have you learned?

We have all experienced such uneasy feelings over simplistic solutions and go-through-the-motion attitudes. We may have satisfied the letter of the law, fulfilling all of the requirements—but in that place within us where God alone resides we are not satisfied, we know things are incomplete, and we seek resolution and purpose. In today's Gospel, Jesus reminds us that compassion transcends legal limits, that reconciliation requires going beyond our own interests and demands for vengeance, and that acting justly and mercifully overcomes anger, opposition, and cynicism.

In the Gospel scheme of things, the human heart is decisive in determining right and wrong. Our faithfulness to reciting certain prayers is meaningless if selfishness and hatred separate us from family and friends; anger is more than an emotion if it sets off of a potentially destructive chain of events in human relationships; sexual immorality cannot be dismissed as mere "failings" when they lead to the degradation of another's dignity and disintegration of a family.

Christ speaks not of rules and regulations but the much deeper and profound values of the human heart.

Meditation: Is there a situation in your life that you have accepted as "the way things are" but could be better resolved or made whole?

Prayer: Risen Christ, may we never hesitate to forgive and seek forgiveness from one another; may we never let hatred, distrust, and disappointment bury us in tombs of self-righteousness and anger—but let the power of your forgiveness take hold in our hearts so that we may transform our families, parishes, and communities in the hope and promise of Easter.

Want Peace? Start With Your Sister . . .

Readings: Deut 26:16-19; Matt 5:43-48

Scripture:
"But I say to you, love your enemies,
   and pray for those who persecute you." (Matt 5:44)

Reflection: In her memoir *Marriage and Other Acts of Charity*, Kate Braestrup writes about reading St. John's letter on love with her little son Peter. She writes:

> God is love . . . . That's a whole theology in three words. The practical application of that theology—*God is love*—is nearly as simple. *Be as loving as you can, as often as you can, for as many people as you can, for as long as you live. Why should you do this? Because.*
>
> It's simple enough for a child to understand. "I can do it," Peter [my son] said stoutly when I explained it to him. "I can be loving toward anyone. Even an ax murderer."
>
> "Start with you sister," I told him.
>
> Start with your spouse. That's what I had to do. Whomever you start with, it doesn't end there. Once I'd gotten the principle more or less down as it applied to [my husband] Drew, it quickly became obvious that the same could apply to other people, and not just the safely distant murderer who has taken the ax to a stranger. The principle

might also apply to the guy who swipes my parking spot at Shop-N-Save, or to the telemarketer who calls at suppertime, or even—imagine this!—to my relatives!

The real challenge of Jesus' teachings on loving one's enemies is not "loving" some group assigned a label based on politics or sociology or economics or "loving" some remote "sinner" we will never have anything to do with. The challenge of today's Gospel is to love the people with whom we live and work and go to school, the people with whom we struggle, the people who annoy us (and, hard to imagine, those whom *we* annoy). The Jesus of the Gospel instills within us a vision that sees beyond stereotypes, politics, and appearances and recognizes and honors the goodness possessed by every human being.

"To love our enemies" is not just to declare a ceasefire but to create and maintain an atmosphere where reconciliation is always possible and actively sought.

Meditation: Who do you find most difficult to "love" and what might be the first step in beginning a relationship or healing the rift between you and that person?

Prayer: In this season of forgiveness, O Lord, may the light of your wisdom enable us to recognize our role in the endless cycle of tension, distrust, anger, and war that destroys our world. Transform our hearts so that we may seek always to be vehicles of forgiveness that heals and transforms. May your Son's spirit of humility and love move our spirits to be ready to love first, despite the cost.

Les Miserables

Readings: Gen 22:1-2, 9a, 10-13, 15-18; Rom 8:31b-34; Mark 9:2-10

Scripture:
[Jesus] was transfigured before them,
 and his clothes became dazzling white,
 such as no fuller on earth could bleach them.
  (Mark 9:2b-3)

Reflection: Victor Hugo's masterwork, *Les Miserables*, begins with a simple but profound moment of forgiveness. Jean Valjean has been imprisoned for stealing a small loaf of bread to feed his sister's daughter. Paroled after 20 years of hard labor and brutal treatment, Valjean is a broken, bitter man. He is desperate for work but no one will hire a parolee. Cold and hungry, he is taken in by a kind bishop.

During the night, Valjean steals the bishop's silver plate and flees, but he is quickly taken into custody by the local police. The constables bring Valjean to the bishop's residence and ask the bishop to identify the thief and his silver. Indeed it is his silver, the Monseigneur says—but the bishop explains that he *gave* Valjean the silver. He thanks the police for bringing Valjean to him because he was concerned that Valjean forgot to take the valuable candlesticks as well.

Valjean is stunned by the bishop's extraordinary kindness and forgiveness. The bishop only asks Valjean to use the silver to re-create his life and return God's goodness to others. "God has raised you out of darkness," the bishop blesses Valjean. "I have bought your soul for God."

The kindness of the bishop is an experience of transfiguration for Valjean. As the three disciples behold the divinity that radiates from the vision of Jesus on the mountaintop, Valjean realizes the ember of God's goodness that has continued to burn within him despite the brutality and cruelty of his two decades in prison. That same touch of divinity exists within each one of us, as well: God is present within us, animating us to do good and holy things; guiding our steps as we try to walk justly and humbly in the ways of God and enlightening our vision with wisdom and selflessness to bring the justice and mercy of God into our world.

Meditation: How can the kindness or forgiveness you offer be the means for transfiguration for someone—as well as for yourself?

Prayer: May the light of your love illuminate our hearts, O God, that we may discover the sense of your divinity within ourselves. May that sacredness enable us to see beyond our own needs, wants and interests so that we may we set about to transfigure our lives and our world in your compassion, justice and forgiveness.

By the Numbers

Readings: Dan 9:4b-10; Luke 6:36-38

Scripture:
"For the measure with which you measure
    will in return be measured out to you." (Luke 6:38)

Reflection: From the moment we memorize the sequence of numbers from one to ten, we play the numbers game.

We measure ourselves and many of our relationships by counting. Children count baseball cards and Beanie Babies. Athletes count every throw, every point, every assist, and every second left on the clock. Business people count billings, expenses, assets, bookings, and the bottom line. Value is measured in terms of the number of dollars and cents—we are "worth" X-number of dollars; are valued at X-number of dollars. Even art is evaluated in numbers: the number of tickets sold, the number of units shipped, the weekly box office gross, the Nielsen ratings, the price the painting brought at auction.

How do we measure success? Through the numbers: through statistics, through the polling data, through profit and loss statements.

The person of faith, however, is called to invest love, caring and compassion in people without looking for a profit. Just as God constantly calls us back despite the many times we reject him, we Christians are called to look beyond numbers to see human beings as brothers and sisters.

In the reign of God, love and mercy are the "bottom line." Jesus calls all of us who would be his disciples to love as God loves us—unconditionally and without limit. And in the end, Jesus assures us, God will "make the numbers work."

Meditation: What values, beliefs, and principles make up the yardstick by which you measure your decisions?

Prayer: Father of compassion, give us the gift of your Spirit of love, gratitude, and forgiveness. Do not let self-interest, judgment, and vengeance measure our lives, but help us to use your rule of love, forgiveness, and justice.

Margaret

Readings: Isa 1:10, 16-20; Matt 23:1-12

Scripture:
"The greatest among you must be your servant."
  (Matt 23:11)

Reflection: Of course there's the pastor, the board, the director, and the head of volunteers—but the heart and soul of the place is Margaret.

Margaret has been part of the soup kitchen and pantry "community" since the day it was organized—first as a "guest," now as a volunteer. Margaret knows how to get the finicky stove to work, when to show up at local supermarkets to get the best leftover food before it is thrown away, how to "stretch" the soup to feed another dozen people. But she also knows the stories—stories of losing a job, of being forced from your home, of having to choose between turning on the heat or buying food, of surviving on the streets. Margaret treats those who come to the parish table with dignity and respect, without patronizing them or judging them.

Every new volunteer works their first shifts with Margaret—and they learn a great deal more form her than how to ladle soup.

In the gospel view of the world, authority is not a matter of power or wealth or education; greatness cannot be measured in terms of celebrity or vote totals. Jesus exalts those whose leadership and influence over others are centered in humble, joyful service, in integrity and selflessness, in respect for the hopes and dreams of others. The "greatness" of Margaret and good women and men like her is centered in a faith-filled vision of the world that honors the holiness of God in everyone.

For those who would be Jesus' disciples, joy is found not in the recognition or honor that one receives in doing good but in the act of doing good itself, in realizing that we imitate Christ in such service, in the assurance that we are bringing the love of God into the lives of others. Jesus, who welcomed to his side the rejected and scorned of society, who washed the feet of his friends and taught them to do the same, leaves the legacy of such "greatness" to us, his church.

Meditation: Who do you know that models the "servant," as described by Jesus in today's Gospel?

Prayer: Father, may we experience the joy of being your servant to others. In whatever good we are able to do, help us to find meaning and fulfillment. In our small, unseen, unheralded acts of compassion and forgiveness, may we reflect your healing and peace in our midst.

March 4: Wednesday of the Second Week of Lent

The Call to Compassion

Readings: Jer 18:18-20, Matt 20:17-28

Scripture:
"[W]hoever wishes to be great among you shall be your
        servant." (Matt 20:26)

Reflection: A friend was visiting the chaplain at a hospice. In
the course of the conversation, the chaplain said that that weekend eight of the hospice's 30 patients had died. The visitor
asked about the effect of so many deaths on the staff. That was
tough, the chaplain said, and shared one particular story.

    That Saturday, a woman who had been at the hospice for
a couple of months had a visit from her teenage son. It was
a great visit, filled with laughs and fun and hugs. At noon
the boy told his mother that he was going to have lunch with
friends but would be back later in the afternoon. But shortly
after the son had left, the mother called the nurse on duty, a
wonderful young woman who was the patient's favorite
nurse of all.

    "I think this is it. I may be dying."

    The nurse checked her vital signs and replied honestly,
"It's possible you are." The patient then asked her friend,
"Will you hold me? I think if you hold me I can do this well."
The young nurse did not hesitate—she cradled her emaciated
body in her arms and held her into eternity.

The visitor than asked the chaplain, "What about the nurse? What did it do to her?" The chaplain replied that the nurse had taken four days off to go to the mountains to think about whether to come back to work.

"Do you think she'll be back?" the chaplain was asked.

"She'll be back. You learn in a place like this that caring hurts. But when you really care you offer something special—and become special yourself."

This young nurse—and the thousands of dedicated medical professionals and caregivers like her—understand that their work of healing and compassion is centered in that extraordinary sense of total, selfless, unconditional, and complete love that is of God. She understands that discipleship—whether lived in ordained ministry or as faithful lay men and women—is a call to be the "servant" envisioned by Jesus, to readily put aside his or her own needs and disappointments to extend Christ's compassion. They seek to provide, regardless of the cost, havens for the lost to return, for the grieving to mourn, for the wounded to heal.

Meditation: In what simple, ordinary ways can you imitate the attitude of Jesus the servant?

Prayer: Father, Source of love, inspire us with your Son's spirit of humility to realize that in our love for others we express our love for you, that in serving others we serve you, and that in giving to others we give thanks to you. Help us to embrace your Son's attitude of joyful servanthood so that we may re-create our lives and world in your life and love.

Lazarus at Your Gate

Readings: Jer 17:5-10; Luke 16:19-31

Scripture:
"There was a rich man who dressed in purple garments
    and fine linen
  and dined sumptuously each day.
And lying at his door was a poor man named Lazarus,
    covered with sores,
who would gladly have eaten his fill of the scraps
  that fell from the rich man's table." (Luke 16:19-21)

Reflection: Look—Lazarus is at your door.

Lazarus is at your door, in desperate need of help in the wake of crippling poverty or hopeless illness.

Lazarus is at your door, hungry for respect and acceptance, wanting only his or her gifts and abilities to be accepted for the common good.

Lazarus is at your door, a victim of bigotry and bullying, distrusted and avoided because he or she is of the wrong social class, follows the wrong religion, was born with the wrong skin color.

Lazarus is at your door, another nameless number lost in a ravaged economy or a broken education system.

Lazarus's struggles go largely unnoticed. Lazarus has no voice. Lazarus's life is a constant fight for meager scraps and leftovers.

But in Lazarus we see God: in his poverty, we realize the many blessings we have received from God; in his suffering, we understand our responsibility that comes with those blessings to lift Lazarus out of his poverty—be it a poverty of spirit, of health, of respect and dignity, or of the basic necessities of life.

Look around today. See Lazarus at your door—and welcome him inside your home and heart.

Meditation: Who are the "Lazaruses" at your own gates, and how can you respond to their plight?

Prayer: Loving God, illuminate our vision to see the poor, the needy, the forgotten at our own gates; open our hearts to welcome them into our lives with compassion and respect. In welcoming the Lazaruses to our tables, may we welcome you; in giving to them from the bounty you have given us, may we give you thanks. Through the Lazaruses we meet and welcome, may we discover your joy in giving to others as you have given to us.

The Legend of Noble Bamboo

Readings: Gen 37:3-4, 12-13a, 17b-28a; Matt 21:33-43, 45-46

Scripture:
"But when the tenants saw the son, they said to one
    another,
  'This is the heir.
Come, let us kill him and acquire his inheritance.'
They seized him, threw him out of the vineyard, and
    killed him." (Matt 21: 38-39)

Reflection: The Thais have a wonderful legend about the
bamboo plant. When the great garden of the earth was first
planted, Bamboo was the most beautiful plant of all, the
favorite flower of the Master of the Garden. In one corner of
the earth there were some dry fields. A spring of water was
in the center of the fields, but its water could not reach the
dry earth.

So the Master of the Garden called his beloved Bamboo
plant, "Noble Bamboo, I would use thee."

And Bamboo replied, "I am ready. Use me as you will."

The Master explained what he was going to do.

Bamboo shook with horror. Bamboo asked that he be spared
the Master's plan, but the Master explained that he had no
choice. Bamboo then bowed before the Master of the Garden
and said, "Do as you must, Master. Use me as you will.

And so the Master of the Garden took Bamboo and cut him down and hacked off his branches and stripped off his leaves, cleaved him in two and cut out his heart. Then the Master gently carried Bamboo to the fresh water spring and, putting one end of broken Bamboo in the spring and the other end into the water channel in the dry field, the Master gently laid down his beloved Bamboo. The clear waters raced down the channel of Bamboo's torn body into the waiting fields. The rice was planted, the shoots grew and the harvest came.

On that day, Bamboo, once so glorious in its stately beauty, became more glorious in his brokenness and humility.

Like the legend of Bamboo, Jesus' life is a story of how a spirit of humble servanthood can transform barrenness into bounty, evil into good, despair into hope, selfishness into justice, death into life. He asks all of us who would be his disciples to embrace the role of servant, emptying ourselves of our own needs and wants and self-importance for the sake of others, realizing the profound truth that we receive only in giving, that greatness is found only in humility and service, that resurrection is possible only in suffering and death.

Meditation: How can you imitate the generosity in the selfless spirit of "noble" Bamboo?

Prayer: Loving God, help us to embrace the example of Bamboo—that in putting aside our own wants and needs, we might build your vineyard of compassion and peace; that in our humble dying to self, we may realize your harvest of new life and hope for all.

"Pig-sty Epiphany"

Readings: Mic 7:14-15, 18-20; Luke 15:1-3, 11-32

Scripture:
"[H]e hired himself out to one of the local citizens
 who sent him to his farm to tend the swine.
And he longed to eat his fill of the pods on which the
  swine fed,
 but nobody gave him anything.
Coming to his senses, he thought,
 'How many of my father's hired workers
 have more than enough to eat,
 but here am I, dying of hunger.'" (Luke 15:15-17)

Reflection: We have all had our "pig-sty epiphanies." We have made a mess of things, and we cannot or refuse to understand how bad of a mess we have made. But eventually there comes that moment when we can no longer deny how much hurt we have caused; we reach the point when we can no longer stand the situation and finally resolve to act. At long last, we bring ourselves to face the mess that our selfishness, our insensitivity, or our dishonesty have made of our lives and the lives of those whom we love. We realize how estranged we've become from ourselves and others; we've had enough of being trapped in the prisons created by our deceptions; we wish to rise from the tombs of fear that we have dug for ourselves.

In today's parable of the Prodigal Son, the moment of conversion takes place when the prodigal, reduced to tending the swine, finally accepts responsibility for the disaster he has made of his life. It is the beginning of his reconciliation with his father and family. Forgiveness's only chance at "sticking" depends on our realizing that we are in need of forgiveness and that such forgiveness—despite our doubts, insecurities, and egos—is possible.

Christ calls us to embrace a spirit of humility that enables us to realize our culpability for the hurt we cause. And he gives a word of hope that enables us to pick ourselves up out of the mud and muck and re-create our lives in reconciliation and forgiveness.

Meditation: When was the last time you admitted to yourself that you had made a mess of something—and how were you able to make things right and whole again?

Prayer: As we travel with you this Lent, O Lord, instill in us your wisdom and humility so that we might lift ourselves out of the mud that bogs us down, turn away from the self-centeredness that makes life difficult for ourselves and those who care about us, and refocus our lives on our journey to your eternal dwelling place.

Turning Over, Driving Out, Unplugging

Readings: Exod 20:1-17; 1 Cor 1:22-25; John 2:13-25

Scripture:
[Jesus] made a whip out of cords
    and drove [the money changers] out of the temple
        area, . . .
    and to those who sold doves he said,
    "Take these out of here,
    and stop making my Father's house a marketplace."
        (John 2:15, 16)

Reflection: He would probably start by grabbing all the iPhones and electronic devices that we bury our faces in and throw them all out a window. He'd then yank us from our couches and smash all the widescreen televisions we vegetate in front of. We'd be stunned as he turned over our wine racks, golf clubs, sports gear, gourmet kitchens, and the infinite number of devices and gadgets that occupy our time.

Enough, Jesus would say. *Life—your life—is holy and you're wasting it away.*

A little harsh, Jesus, we might dare to say.

Maybe. But his angry toppling of the vendors' booths ringing the temple court confronts us with how we desecrate our lives with possessions and obsessions that displace what should be the focus of our lives. In today's Gospel, Jesus drives out all of those things that undermine the mission and ministry of God's house: the commerce that diminishes prayer and currency exchanges that distort the meaning of sacrifice.

Jesus challenges us: What distracts us from living a life of purpose and meaning? What monopolizes our time and energy at the expense of those we love? What enables us to avoid the difficult work of reconciliation, justice, and mercy?

Not that any of these things are bad in themselves, but when they become the center of our lives, crutches we cannot bear to be without, obsessions that steal away the precious gift of time, it's time to clean out the temple.

Lent (which comes from the old English word for *springtime*) is the time for a "spring cleaning" of our spirits and souls: for driving out of our lives the useless, the meaningless, and the destructive. Lent is a time to invite the "angry" Jesus of today's Gospel into our lives to drive out those things that make our lives less than what God created them to be.

And he'll probably start with your phone.

Meditation: What device or activity in your life might be monopolizing too much of your time at the expense of more important things?

Prayer: Lord of Easter newness, drive out of our homes and hearts the unnecessary and the useless that clutter our lives and monopolize our time. Restore our spirits to a sense of perspective that enables us to use the wonders of creation and technology to realize the meaning and purpose of our lives. May these days of Lent be a "spring cleaning" of those things that clutter and "muddy" our relationships with you and one another.

March 9: Monday of the Third Week of Lent

Prophetess of Bread

Readings: 2 Kgs 5:1-15b, Luke 4:24-30

Scripture:
"No prophet is accepted in his own native place."
(Luke 4:24)

Reflection: English writer and retreat leader Margaret Silf recounts the following:

> During World War II, it was reported, a battered contingent of defeated allied soldiers was being paraded through a German village. The streets were lined with onlookers, some with triumph on their faces, others with compassion. The prisoners were starving and utterly exhausted, their eyes cast down in despair. A silence fell. Then a woman broke through, an ordinary German housewife, and thrust a loaf of bread into one of the prisoner's hands before fleeing back to her kitchen. She took the risk of compassionate action. She stepped out of line. But she also started a movement. Gradually others overcame their fears and brought out food for the captives. One woman's action caused thousands to be fed.

One woman's prophetic act of courageous generosity resulted in the transformation of enemy soldiers into sons and brothers. To act prophetically begins by embracing what is right and just and then being willing to confront whatever evil seeks to destroy that good. In baptism, all of us are called to be ministers of such goodness, however unpopular that may make us and regardless of the cost such prophesy exacts from us.

Lent reminds us that we are all called to be such prophets. Most of the opportunities we have to prophetic proclamation are quiet, ordinary, and unseen—perhaps having no discernible effect beyond our immediate families. But we can still bring a measure of hope to others in the sincerity, kindness, and joy we bring to the everyday dimensions of life. No matter how we live and fulfill that "prophetic role" ourselves, the challenge is the same: to persevere in our belief that the God we "proclaim"—the God of compassion, justice and reconciliation—is so much greater than the promises and demands of the world in which we struggle to make our way.

Meditation: Consider the ways you are able to "proclaim" or "prophesy" God's presence in the midst of your family or community.

Prayer: O God, in the waters of baptism, in the breaking of bread, you send us forth to be your prophets. Give us the grace and courage to proclaim your presence in our midst. May every kindness, every act of forgiveness, every moral and ethical stand we take be our voice as your prophets, proclaiming your love, mercy, and justice to all your sons and daughters.

Sometimes a Parent Can Surprise You

Readings: Dan 3:25, 34-43; Matt 18:21-35

Scripture:
"So will my heavenly Father do to you,
  unless each of you forgives your brother from your
    heart." (Matt 18:35)

Reflection: The teenager had her driver's license for only a few weeks. After much pleading, Dad relented and let her use the family's new car to take her friends to the beach.

She was very careful. She kept under the speed limit the whole time. She took great pains to park the car in a safe spot.

But on the trip home, *crunch!* She never saw the other car. In an instant, the front bumper, headlight, and part of the door became a crumbled mass of metal.

She wanted to die. Dad would have her head. *Might as well burn my driver's license,* she thought. *I'll be grounded for life.*

And so she limped home in her father's once beautiful car, terrified at the consequences to come.

As she pulled into the driveway, her parents were waiting in the doorway. When they saw her drive up, they ran outside. From the looks on their faces, she knew this would not be a happy homecoming. Dad ran ahead of Mom—and right past the damage. He took his daughter's hand and helped her out of the car.

46 *Tuesday of the Third Week of Lent*

"Dad, I'm sorry . . . ," she stammered.

But he wouldn't let her finish.

"Are you all right? Were you hurt? Was anybody hurt?" he wanted to know, hugging her tighter and tighter.

She began to cry—a little surprised that her Dad was so understanding—and a little ashamed that she had expected so little from him.

We've all had similar experiences. Just when we expected to pay the price for hurting and letting someone down, they responded with understanding, compassion, and immediate forgiveness. So it is with God, who always welcomes us back to him without condition or limit.

The great mystery of faith is that God continues to love us, continues to call us back to him, continues to help us repair the damage we cause. All God asks of us is that we forgive one another as he forgives us, that we lift up those who stumble as God lifts us up when we stumble, that we help those in trouble clean up the messes they make of their lives as God helps us clean up our own messes.

Meditation: What do you find to be the biggest obstacle to forgiving someone who hurts you?

Prayer: Loving Father, help us to let go of our angers and resentments, our embarrassments and disappointments, in order to begin repairing our brokenness with others and with you. By your grace, may we transform the darkness and cold of our winters into the warmth and light of Easter by seeking forgiveness and reconciliation with all who hurt us and whom we have hurt.

In Praise of That One Teacher

Readings: Deut 4:1, 5-9; Matt 5:17-19

Scripture:
"[W]hoever obeys and teaches these commandments
   will be called greatest in the Kingdom of heaven."
      (Matt 5:19)

Reflection: Most of us have had that one great teacher who taught us not just by instruction but by enthusiasm for the subject.

Some of us have had a boss who became a mentor, who showed us not just how the business worked but how to succeed in the workplace.

And many of us have worked with someone who led by example, who inspired us by his or her own tireless dedication to the cause and the importance of the work you were taking on.

In today's Gospel, Jesus honors such teachers, mentors, and leaders and calls on all who would be his disciples to the work of teaching through example, of inspiring through sacrifice, of leading through service.

In our lives as loving parents, in the ethics and justice we bring to the workplace, in our most hidden generosity and charity we "teach" the Gospel of God's Christ and "lead" in the establishment of the Father's kingdom in the here and now.

Meditation: Who has been your most inspiring teacher or most generous mentor in matters of faith?

Prayer: Thank you, O God, for the many gifted teachers and generous mentors and leaders who have taught us in our lives. Inspired by their dedication and wisdom, may we teach and lead others along the common path we all follow to your dwelling place.

March 12: Thursday of the Third Week of Lent

Party Hardy

Readings: Jer 7:23-28, Luke 11:14-23

Scripture:
"Every kingdom divided against itself will be laid waste and house will fall against house." (Luke 11:17)

Reflection: There is an old African folk tale about a mighty chief who planned a great feast and invited the entire village. All were eager to attend, but there was one stipulation. The chief would furnish all the food and entertainment, but each of those invited had to bring a jug of wine. It would be poured into one huge vat and then there would be plenty for all.

One villager did not have any wine and was too miserly to buy a jug. "There must be a way to go without having to buy wine," he thought to himself. Then he struck upon an idea. "With so many others bringing wine to pour into the vat, no will notice if I just put water in my jug and pour it in. With such a great amount of wine, one jar of water will hardly be noticed."

So on the day of the festival, the villagers, dressed in their finest clothes, made their way to the chief's banquet. As each guest arrived, they poured the contents of their jars into the great basin. All paid their respects to the chief and joined the party.

When the chief saw that everyone had arrived, he interrupted the music and dancing to welcome everyone. Then he announced that the time had come for the first toast. The chief ordered the glasses filled with wine from the vat. All raised their glasses to their lips and drank.

But there was something strange about the wine. The puzzled chief drank again. He did not taste wine—but water! Each villager had the same idea: that his jug of water would not spoil such a huge basin of wine. They received what they gave.

The chief was angry beyond words and had his guards banish the selfish villagers from his land forever.

Jesus invites every one of us, not to accomplish great things, but to give willingly of whatever we have for the sake of the common good. The measure of faithful discipleship is not the quality and amount of "wine" we give, but the Spirit of generosity and joy that compels us to give the best wine we have.

The kingdom of God will be established on such humble selflessness, while self-interest and greed will reduce our homes and churches and communities to lifeless, arid deserts.

Meditation: What small, ordinary contribution of yours would make your home or community or parish a happier, more loving place?

Prayer: Lord Jesus, cast out selfishness and arrogance. In their place, ignite your Spirit of compassion and selflessness from our hearts that we may make of our own homes and villages holy places of welcome, forgiveness, and justice.

March 13: Friday of the Third Week of Lent

Blood Brother

Readings: Hos 14:2-10; Mark 12:28-34

Scripture:
You shall love the Lord your God with all your heart,
   with all your soul,
   with all your mind,
   and with all your strength. . . .
   You shall love your neighbor as yourself.
There is no other commandment greater than these.
      (Mark 12:29-30, 31)

Reflection: In her book *Bird by Bird: Some Instructions on Writing and Life*, Anne Lamott calls this "the best true story on giving I know":

An eight-year-old boy had a younger sister who was dying of leukemia. His parents explained to him that she needed a blood transfusion and that his blood was probably compatible. He agreed to have his blood tested, and the tests showed that his blood was compatible to his sister's. Mom and Dad asked their son if he would give his sister a pint of blood. The boy asked if he could think about it overnight. Lamott writes:

"The next day he went to his parents and said he was ready to donate his blood. So they took him to the hospital where he was put on a gurney beside his sister. Both of them were hooked up to IVs. A nurse withdrew a pint of blood from the boy, which was then put into the girl's IV. The boy lay on his gurney in silence while his blood dripped into his sister, until the doctor came over to see how he was doing. The boy opened his eyes and asked, 'How soon I until I start to die?'"

Every word of Jesus' gospel comes down to love: love that is simple enough to articulate but so demanding that we shy away from it. The mystery of God's love is that the Being of supreme and omnipotent power should love his creation so completely and so selflessly—and all God seeks in return is that such love be shared by his people throughout his creation.

The brother, believing that giving his blood would mean he would die, nonetheless was willing to give his life to his little sister so that she might live; in his generosity, he modeled the great love and compassion of the God who spares nothing to bring us to him.

Meditation: What is the most complete expression of love you have ever experienced—and how have you expressed your love for another totally and without reservation?

Prayer: Father, you are the source and center of our lives. Filled with wonder at the world you have fashioned and humbled with gratitude at the depth of your loving generosity, may we use every moment and ability you have given us to re-create and restore this time and place in your compassion and peace.

"The Last Emperor"

Readings: Hos 6:1-6; Luke 18:9-14

Scripture:
"[F]or everyone who exalts himself will be humbled,
and the one who humbles himself will be exalted."
(Luke 18:14)

Reflection: The 1987 epic film *The Last Emperor* is the true story of Puyi, the last emperor of China. As a boy, Puyi is revered as the "Son of Heaven," revered and honored by his subjects as a god. The boy was protected from the world outside his beautiful palace, for his people considered him to be the center of their nation and world.

But the young emperor's world of privilege comes crashing down in the Communist revolution in the mid-1930s. Puyi is forced to flee his opulent life in the Forbidden City. In his dangerous exile, the deposed emperor discovers that he is not divine but very human, that he is not superior to others but their equal in dignity and purpose, subject to the same doubts and insecurities and fears. His humility leads him to discover who he is and what his life can and should be about. The loss of his luxurious, isolated existence becomes for Puyi a victory for discovering a meaningful life of kindness and generosity.

True humility is the grace to see beyond our own needs and dreams to realize that everyone—man and woman, young and old, Christian and Jew, believer and nonbeliever, black and white—is made in the image and likeness of God and therefore worthy of respect and dignity as a child of God. The Pharisee's prayer—and "separateness"—is empty before God, while the tax collector's prayer, in its simple humility, is heard by God. The self-righteousness of the Pharisee can be destructive and isolating while the tax collector's acceptance of his own need for mercy and forgiveness can be the beginning of healing and resurrection.

Jesus challenges us to embrace the humble, God-centered faith of the tax collector, not the self-centered claims of the Pharisee. We give thanks for God's love for us by returning that love to one another, by accepting each other as God has accepted us; we honor God as Father of us all by honoring everyone as our brothers and sisters.

Meditation: What has been the most difficult but revealing lesson in humility that you have learned?

Prayer: Gracious God, your Son taught us to call you Father and one another brother and sister. Help us to realize that we are all members of one human family. May we embrace the humility that heals and the peace of the gospel that rejoices in you as Father of us all.

March 15: Fourth Sunday of Lent

"Mid-faith"

Readings: 2 Chr 36:14-16, 19-23; Eph 2:4-10; John 3:14-21

Scripture:
"[W]hoever lives the truth comes to the light,
    so that his works may be clearly seen as done in God."
        (John 3:21)

Reflection: In her memoir *Still: Notes on a Mid-Faith Crisis*, Lauren Winner writes about her life after her conversion from Judaism to Christianity and her struggle to continue to seek God in the midst of her divorce and the death of her mother. Winner, who teaches at Duke Divinity School, writes:

"The enthusiasms of my conversion have worn off. . . . Since [my] baptism, my belief has faltered, my sense of God's closeness has grown strained, my efforts at living in accord with what I take to be the call of the gospel have come undone.

"And yet in those same moments of strained belief, of not knowing where or if God is, it has also seemed that the Christian story keeps explaining who and where I am, better than any other story I know. On the days when I think I have a fighting chance at redemption, at change, I understand it to be these words and these rituals and these people who will change me. Some days I am not sure if my faith is riddled with doubt or whether, graciously, my doubt is riddled with faith. . . . I doubt; I am uncertain; I am restless, prone to wander. And yet glimmers of holy keep interrupting my gaze."

Winner writes that we all come to a spiritual "middle" in our lives: the griefs, failures, and disappointments bring us to a point where we think God is absent. We are exhausted from struggling to hear God in the noise of our lives and trying to find him amid all the expectations and demands made of us. What we need to keep in mind is that our baptismal conversion from darkness to light, as Jesus describes in today's Gospel, is an ongoing journey. Our search for God *begins* at baptism, it does not end there. The challenge is to keep our hearts and spirits open to the presence of God, to intentionally—and stubbornly—realize God's presence in prayer, in whatever good we can do, in the love and support of family and friends.

In "mid-faith," when we feel most alone, when we feel furthest from God, God invariably makes his presence known.

Meditation: Have you ever been surprised to discover God in your midst when God seemed most absent?

Prayer: O God, may we embrace the perspective of faith and attitude of hope your Son revealed to Nicodemus. By your light, may we realize your presence even in our darkest nights. By your grace, help us to persevere in faith despite our exhaustion and hurt. By your Spirit of compassion and forgiveness, heal our broken spirits into hearts made whole.

March 15: Fourth Sunday of Lent **57**

March 16: Monday of the Fourth Week of Lent

Missed Signs

Readings: Isa 65:17-21; John 4:43-54

Scripture:
"Unless you people see signs and wonders, you will not
  believe." (John 4:48)

Reflection: We track the numbers: How is your portfolio
doing? Is that IPO a good deal?

We watch trends: How is your company's product faring
in the marketplace? How are ticket sales? Is that cold front
going to affect your weekend plans? Can he hit left-handed
pitching?

We study what we can barely see: Do the lab results indi-
cate cancer?

We are always watching for signs and grasping at indica-
tors to help us decide what to do, what to buy, how to respond. Our faces are buried in video screens of all shapes
and sizes, looking for that sign that could mean wealth, success, victory.

In today's Gospel, people have been begging Jesus for
more signs that he is the Messiah. But they miss the perfect
sign of God in their midst: a father's love for his dying child.

These Lenten days challenge us to look up from the numbers flying across our screens and spread sheets and pay
attention to the real signs of God in our midst: the love of

family and friends, the kindness and goodness we are able to give and receive, the forgiveness that heals and mends.

Meditation: What clear "sign" of God's presence do you often overlook in your life?

Prayer: Open our hearts, O God, to perceive the signs of your presence in our lives. In a spirit of humility and gratitude, may we see your hand in every wonder of creation, hear your voice in the cry of the poor and struggling who call out to us, feel your loving embrace in the compassion and forgiveness of those we love.

Walk Around

Readings: Ezek 47:1-9, 12; John 5:1-16

Scripture:
"Sir, I have no one to put me into the pool
when the water is stirred up." (John 5:7)

Reflection: For the 38 years he had been confined to his mat, his paralysis made it impossible to maneuver on his own. His one hope was that someone—anyone—would see him and have enough pity to help him into the pool at the Sheep Gate, a spring of water that was believed to hold healing powers.

Perhaps the real wonder in this Gospel is not so much that Jesus healed the man but that Jesus *saw* the man. And perhaps the real reason the Jewish elders were angry with Jesus was not that he healed the paralyzed man on the Sabbath but that he healed him at all—as if this insignificant man was worth their time, their energy, and their attention.

"Sir, I have no one to put me into the pool."

How pathetic, how sad—not for the paralyzed man, but for those who passed by him every day, those who could not or would not see him or acknowledge him. How many people must have just about tripped over him on their way through the porticoes?

How pathetic, how sad are we—who walk by, who walk around, who walk looking straight ahead, ignoring the paralyzed who are struggling to reach the waters of healing, mercy, and dignity. Every day we see the sick, the poor, the troubled who are confined to their mats—they are our children, our classmates and teammates, our coworkers and employees, our neighbors and parishioners. They reach out for the hand of Christ—our hand—to help them rise from their mats and walk with dignity and joy.

Meditation: Is there someone in your life in need of help or recognition whom you have purposely avoided? Why? How can you bring some sense of healing or reconciliation to his or her life?

Prayer: Christ the Healer, help us to see the infirm and paralyzed in our midst. Do not let us ignore them or walk around them. May your love enable us to bend down to help them up, bring them to the waters of your grace and reconciliation, console and comfort them with your word of healing and hope.

"The Minister's Black Veil"

Readings: Isa 49:8-15; John 5:17-30

Scripture:
"[T]he hour is coming and is now here,
    when the dead will hear the voice of the Son of God,
    and those who hear will live." (John 5:25)

Reflection: In a tale by Nathaniel Hawthorne, the congregation of a small New England church is stunned one Sunday morning when their respected young minister, the Reverend Mr. Hooper, enters the church wearing a veil of black crepe over his face. The veil has a chilling effect on the congregation. The minister conducts the service as usual, making no reference to the veil—but its very presence evokes much fear, anxiety, mistrust, and wild speculation among parishioners.

A deputation confronts Hooper about the veil and his reasons for continuing to wear it. The minister answers simply, "If I hide my face for sorrow, there is cause enough, and if I cover it for secret sin, what mortal might not do the same?"

And for the rest of his long life, "Father" Hooper refuses to take off the veil. His congregation eventually comes to accept the veil and their esteem for him and respect for his ministry grows. But even on his deathbed, when an attending minister tries to remove it, the elderly minister, though sick and confused, continues to clutch the veil tightly to his face.

"Why do you tremble for me alone?" he cries. "Tremble also at each other! Have men avoided me, and women shown me no pity, and children screamed and fled, only for my black veil?

"I look around me, and lo! on every visage a Black Veil!"

We cover and surround ourselves with "black veils"—veils of fear, mistrust, prejudice and ignorance that prevent us from living life in the complete joy of God. The Christ of Easter removes those veils once and for all; he calls us forth from the tombs in which we seal ourselves off from others. Our faith in the Easter promise shatters any pretense or rationalization to don those veils again. In raising his Son from the dead, God raises us up as well, no longer "dead" in despair and cynicism but alive in the hope and joy of God's love.

Meditation: What "veil" do you hide behind to avoid difficult situations that make you uncomfortable?

Prayer: Father, help us to hear and speak your word of hope when all seems to be dead in our lives; be our strength to do your work of reconciliation and mercy when such efforts seem impossible and pointless. By your grace, may we bring Easter resurrection into lives veiled in sadness and hopelessness, lives mired in tombs of despair and cynicism.

Joseph the Just

Readings: 2 Sam 7:4-5a, 12-14a, 16; Rom 4:13, 16-18, 22; Matt 1:16, 18-21, 24a or Luke 2:41-51a

Scripture:
Joseph [Mary's] husband, since he was a righteous man,
    yet unwilling to expose her to shame,
    decided to divorce her quietly. (Matt 1:19)

Reflection: He is never quoted in the script. He is always in the background—where he seems quite content to remain—and only comes center stage when there is trouble. Then he suddenly disappears from the story altogether.

All we know about him is found in the one line from Matthew's Gospel: because Joseph was a "righteous man," he decided to divorce Mary discreetly so as not to shame her.

Yet that one morsel of information tells us everything we need to know. Joseph was a "righteous" man: a carpenter, he knew what hard work was, he knew what it meant to support a family, he knew how to keep a small business going. He conducted his affairs with "righteousness"—that is, with justice, integrity, and humility.

Joseph was a man of compassion and decency. When Mary was discovered to be pregnant, he refused to expose her to the full fury of the Law—which could have meant her death.

Instead, he put aside whatever anger and hurt he felt and planned to "divorce her quietly." Joseph was a man of compassion.

As the story continues, Joseph was the loving provider and fearless protector of his wife and child.

Although the traditional language of church dogma qualifies his relationship with Jesus as that of "foster father," make no mistake: Jesus must have learned a great deal about integrity and compassion from his dad. It is not hard to imagine that many of Jesus' teachings and stories in his adult years were inspired in part by the lessons and example of his carpenter father.

May we embrace the "righteousness" of Joseph the Just: to be men and women of integrity and justice, of faithfulness and trust. And may we be inspired by the example of his compassion and decency, imitating his humility in putting aside our own hurts and doubts, our fears and anxieties to be loving spouses, protective parents, and rocks of stability for our families.

Meditation: When have you found yourself having to make a choice between being "right" or compassionate?

Prayer: O God, may we be inspired by the selfless compassion and unwavering devotion of Joseph so that we may likewise be "righteous" within our own families. In times of crisis and tension, bless our families with the hope of your consolation and forgiveness; in times of joy and growth, bless us with a spirit of gratitude, never forgetting that you are the Father of us all, the Giver of all that is good.

March 20: Friday of the Fourth Week of Lent

A Moveable Feast

Readings: Wis 2:1a, 12-22; John 7:1-2, 10, 25-30

Scripture:
Jesus moved about within Galilee;
   he did not wish to travel in Judea,
   because the Jews were trying to kill him.
But the Jewish feast of Tabernacles was near. (John 7:1-2)

Reflection: Today's Gospel takes place during the Jewish feast of Tabernacles. Even though we read this Gospel during the springtime of Lent, the scene actually takes place in the late summer or fall.

The feast of Tabernacles is one of the most joyous and popular celebrations on the Jewish calendar. Also known as the feast of Booths or *Sukkoth*, it is comparable to our American Thanksgiving: at Sukkoth, the Jewish community gives thanks for the gifts of the harvest.

For the celebration, a family or household will construct its own outdoor "booth," a temporary tent or structure in which family and friends gather for the feast. These temporary booths are reminders to Jews of the journey of their ancestors in the 40-year Exodus in the Sinai, from slavery to fulfillment as the people of God.

Lent reminds us of the impermanence of our own lives—that we are on our own journey through the Sinai of time to the dwelling place of God. And along this journey we have much to be grateful for, as God is with us in the love of family and friends, the gifts and blessings of life, and this good earth.

This Lenten day, look within the booth of your own life and see Christ dwelling in your midst.

Meditation: As you continue your Lenten journey, what do you have to be grateful for this Easter that you tend to overlook?

Prayer: Be with us, Lord Jesus, on our Lenten journey. May the realization of your love in our midst transform our lives in your spirit of gratitude and selfless humility so that we may make our way to your Father's dwelling place in the company of family and friends.

The Magnifying Glass

Readings: Jer 11:18-20; John 7:40-53

Scripture:
[A] division occurred in the crowd because of [Jesus].
Some of them even wanted to arrest him,
  but no one laid hands on him. (John 7:43-44)

Reflection: There was once a wealthy merchant who purchased a powerful magnifying glass. He was fascinated with the instrument. Looking through its lens at crystals and flower petals, he was captivated by the beauty and detail it revealed.

The merchant spent many enjoyable hours with the magnifying glass until, one evening, he placed under the lens a morsel of the food he was about to eat for dinner. He was horrified to see the disgusting, monstrous-looking organisms crawling in it—and this particular food he loved. He agonized over what to do. Finally, he concluded that there was only one way out of his dilemma.

He picked up a mallet and shattered the glass to pieces.

Like the powerful magnifying glass that reveals more than the merchant wants to see, Jesus comes to proclaim a gospel that is more than we bargained for. The reign of God that Jesus proclaims is founded on a concept of justice and an attitude of reconciliation that scares us, that threatens the safe, isolated cocoons we have created for ourselves, that shatters our self-centered approach to the world.

To those who really understood him, Jesus' teachings did not suggest comfort and joy. They objected to him as a dangerous firebrand, an idealistic radical who had no grasp of reality or the complexities of the world.

And it's true: Jesus' gospel is not one of comfort, at least to the comfortable. It is not a gospel of peace to those at war with themselves and those around them. Nor is it a gospel of love to those who are concerned only with themselves. Love your enemies and pray for them, invite to your table the poor and those who in no way can repay you, forgive seventy times seven, seek the lowest place, take up your cross and follow—these are dangerous, radical, and subversive teachings that undermine our lifestyles and threaten what the world holds dear.

Better to destroy the glass than be overwhelmed by the vision we see.

Meditation: What single teaching of Christ do you try to "overlook"?

Prayer: Christ Jesus, open our hearts and spirits to behold your vision of the Father's reign, despite our doubts and fears. Be our courage and strength as we cope with those obstacles that isolate us from you. Walk with us as we struggle to become your disciples: sons and daughters of your Father and brothers and sisters to one another.

Sugaring Season

Readings: Jer 31:31-34; Heb 5:7-9; John 12:20-33

Scripture:
"[U]nless a grain of wheat falls to the ground and dies,
   it remains just a grain of wheat;
   but if it dies, it produces much fruit.
Whoever loves his life loses it,
   and whoever hates his life in this world
   will preserve it for eternal life." (John 12:24-25)

Reflection: In many parts of the northern United States and southern Canada, this is "sugaring season." For six weeks, usually from late February through mid-April, maple trees are "tapped" for their sap. During the annual "sap run," the frozen sap in the maple tree thaws and begins to build up pressure within the tree. When the internal pressure reaches a certain point, sap will flow out of any fresh opening or cut.

Farmers and producers collect the crystal-clear sap, then boil it down in an evaporator over a blazing hot fire. Nothing is added; only water is removed. The sap becomes more concentrated until it becomes maple syrup.

The best thing that ever happened to stack of pancakes or French toast begins as a crystal clear sap that thaws in the warmth of the long-awaited spring.

Like the grain of wheat in today's Gospel, maple syrup is a "natural" parable as to what it means to allow ourselves to change, to be re-created in the love of God. In letting our self-centeredness be boiled away, we can transform our lives in the grace and peace of God. In moving beyond anger and disappointments, our fears and skepticism, we can make this a season of healing and hope for ourselves and those we love.

Learn the lesson of the grain of wheat, that we may die to ourselves in order to realize the fruit of God's harvest of justice and forgiveness. Embrace the faith of the spring maple tree, that we may be willing to give of ourselves for the sake of others as Christ gave himself up for us, allowing ourselves to be transformed in the life and love of the Easter Christ.

Meditation: What changes are you facing in your life that scare you the most? How can you face those changes in a spirit of hope?

Prayer: Christ our Redeemer, may we embrace the faith of the grain of wheat: that we may willingly die to our own wants, needs, and fears in order to experience the life of your resurrection in our families, homes, schools, and communities. May we take up own our crosses in your spirit of selflessness and compassion, that we may transform our lives in the complete joy of Easter.

Happy Anniversary

Readings: Dan 13:1-9, 15-17, 19-30, 33-62 or 13:41c-62; John 8:1-11

Scripture:
"Let the one among you who is without sin
be the first to throw a stone at her." (John 8:7)

Reflection: A husband and wife, both 40, were celebrating their fifteenth wedding anniversary. On the couple's special day, an angel came to them and said that, because they had been so devoted to each other, God had sent the angel to grant each of them one wish.

The wife wished for a trip around the world. *Whoosh!* Immediately she had cruise tickets in her hand.

Then it was the husband's turn. He looked at his loving wife. He looked at the tickets. Then, with a devilish twinkle in his eyes, he asked the angel for a much younger female companion.

And *whoosh!* The man suddenly turned 75.

Much to his surprise, the self-absorbed husband discovers that bringing joy and playfulness into his relationship with his wife is as much his responsibility as hers. The same is true of faith: true conversion must begin within ourselves. The key moment in today's Gospel comes when Jesus challenges the woman's accusers to face their own sinfulness before taking on hers; the moral and just world they demand will not begin with their stoning of this woman, but by first confronting their own culpability and failings.

We cannot take on the demons of the world until we confront the demons in our own hearts; we cannot pass sentence on others until we judge our own lives; we cannot change what is beyond us until we repair what is broken within us; we cannot lift up the fallen until we realize that we too are stumbling.

Meditation: What can you change in your own life that might lead to change or re-creation in your family, community, workplace, or parish?

Prayer: Father of forgiveness, make us a people of compassion. Do not let us be blinded by the disappointments and hurts that cause us to reject others, but open our hearts to recognize and welcome the good every one possesses. Give us the courage to reach out to those who fall along the road we travel, so that we may transform what is evil into the reflection of your love. Humble us with your grace to seek forgiveness when we fall, that we may replace the hurt we have caused with healing and reconciliation.

God's Place "Below"

Readings: Num 21:4-9; John 8:21-30

Scripture:
"You belong to what is below,
　I belong to what is above.
You belong to this world,
　but I do not belong to this world." (John 8:23)

Reflection: Every evening you and your family gather around the table for supper. The entree might be some epicurean delight from the pages of *Bon Appétit*—but more often than not, it's Chinese takeout or pizza. As everyone digs in, the table buzzes with talk of tomorrow's soccer game, a crabby teacher, the latest fix-up project, today's office crises, a new knock-knock joke. Here at the kitchen table, parent and child give and receive encouragement, consolation, forgiveness, and love. Especially love. Your kitchen—the place where God is always present.

A storm devastates a town; a fire reduces a neighborhood to burnt timber and ashes; an act of terrorism cuts a wide and bloody swath through a community. That's when they go to work: skilled medical professionals, tireless construction workers, patient and gifted counselors, selfless volunteers. These dedicated souls work around the clock to care for those hurt and injured, rescue those in danger, help the traumatized cope, and begin the hard work of rebuilding. By their very presence, these good people transform the debris and ashes into the kingdom of God.

The tired old downtown building has seen better days but no better use. The city's churches have worked together to turn the brick structure into a community center, a safe place where children can come to play, receive tutoring, or just hang out after school. The well-stocked pantry provides for dozens of hungry families every week; a free clinic offers basic on-site medical care and referral services to the poor and uninsured. Its meeting rooms are always busy: the elderly have a place to go for companionship and immigrants are taught how to master the language of their new homeland. In this austere brick building, God reigns.

The "things" above are not confined to the realm of heaven. What is "above" can be brought into our world "below," transforming even the most ordinary and simple into the kingdom of God. Our journey with Christ this Lent is a time to rediscover the many ways we re-create our world "below" in the joy and hope of Easter.

Meditation: When and where do you experience the presence of God—the "world above"—in your everyday life here in the "world below"?

Prayer: Lord God, help us to appreciate the things of "above" and not be satisfied with the things of "below." Transform our attitudes, enlighten our vision, and instill in us your wisdom so that we may bring the peace and justice of your world "above" to our world and lives here "below."

Mary's Lenten Journey

Readings: Isa 7:10-14; 8:10; Heb 10:4-10; Luke 1:26-38

Scripture:
"Behold, I am the handmaid of the Lord.
May it be done to me according to your word." (Luke 1:38)

Reflection: This season of Lent began with the Spirit leading us into the wilderness of our souls to discover God.

It can be a difficult trip. It means confronting our fears and doubts, our failures and disappointments, our despair and cynicism. A good Lent, however, ends with a new understanding of ourselves, a resolve to change and grow, a conversion of heart and spirit. Our Lenten desert experience may change course or adapt to new circumstances, but it is only completed when we come to the dwelling place of God.

Today, Mary of Nazareth begins her journey in the desert of her own heart. The journey is set in motion when God calls her to give birth to the Christ. She confronts her doubts, her inadequacies, and her confusion; but, with faith in God's grace, she says yes.

Mary's road takes her to be with Elizabeth, to Bethlehem with her beloved Joseph, to the temple to present her newborn to God. Along the way she experiences joy and sorrow, loss and anguish, terror and death. She travels with her son from Nazareth to Jerusalem, from Jerusalem to Golgotha, from the cross to the tomb.

Mary's journey mirrors our own. As parents and spouses ourselves, we have traveled Mary's Lenten road; we have struggled with our own "annunciations" of God in our midst; we have doubted our own abilities and worthiness to "give birth" to Christ in our own lives. But Gabriel's promise of God's compassion and grace to Mary is made to all of us, as well. God calls us to "give birth" to his Christ in our own Nazareths, to be vehicles of salvation and hope in our homes and communities.

Today's Solemnity of the Annunciation—nine months before Christmas—is the perfect Marian feast for Lent, these forty days when our hearts and spirits are especially opened to the presence of Gabriel's announcement that the Lord is with us, that we have nothing to fear, that we have been called by God to be bearers of his Christ.

Meditation: To what "new" places is the Spirit leading you this Lent and how does Mary's journey help you negotiate this new terrain?

Prayer: Gracious God, may we possess the faith and trust of your daughter Mary to say "yes" to your calling us to make your presence known in our time and place. May this Lenten season be a time for discerning your "annunciations" to us to bring your Son into our own homes and hearts.

Gravity

Readings: Gen 17:3-9; John 8:51-59

Scripture:
"[W]hoever keeps my word will never see death."
(John 8:51)

Reflection: *Gravity* is a dazzling and exhilarating film about the majesty and horror of outer space. Dr. Ryan Stone (Sandra Bullock) is a researcher-turned-astronaut who accompanies a space shuttle crew to repair the Hubble telescope. While she is working on the telescope outside the shuttle, a blizzard of space debris from an exploded satellite suddenly hurtles toward them. The shuttle is destroyed and the crew is killed. Stone alone survives; she is now adrift in space and begins a heart-racing odyssey to return to earth.

The key to appreciating the film is the title: *Gravity*. On one level, the movie is a first-rate adventure story about survival in the cruel environment of outer space. Stone is trapped in a silent, dark, unmerciful vacuum and must use all of her training and wit to survive.

But she also struggles with the same absence of "gravity" in her life on earth. The death of her daughter in a schoolyard accident has left her spiritually adrift, alone and helpless, unmoored and unconnected to anyone.

At one point it appears that time has run out. Death is imminent. The moment is an epiphany: "I know we're all going to die—but I'm going to die today. Funny to know (that), but the thing is that I'm still scared. I'm really scared. Nobody will mourn for me, nobody will pray for my soul."

Imagining that she is speaking to someone who might hear her last words, she asks aloud, "Will you mourn for me? Will you say a prayer for me? Or is it too late? I'd say one for myself, but I've never prayed in my life. Nobody ever taught me how. Nobody ever taught me how."

Gravity evokes those times every one of us experiences in our lives, whether in the vastness of space or on the hard ground of earth, when hope seems lost and to continue on would be pointless—yet somehow we find a reason to persevere. Through grace, we rediscover "gravity": a connectedness to love, a rootedness in compassion, a lifeline of grace. In Christ, we experience such gravity in the healing, compassion, and forgiveness we encounter in our travels.

Meditation: In what situations or relationships do you feel "adrift"? How can you restore a sense of "gravity" to those circumstances?

Prayer: God of all time and space, open our spirits to embrace your vision of the world—a universe that is complete and holy, a world that is sustained by your hand, a human family in which you breathe your life into the souls of all. Centered in the "gravity" of your mercy and compassion, may we re-create our world in the new life of Easter joy.

Who You are NOT

Readings: Jer 20:10-13; John 10:31-42

Scripture:
"If [the law] calls them gods to whom the word of God
     came,
   and Scripture cannot be set aside,
   can you say that the one
   whom the Father has consecrated and sent into the
     world
   blasphemes because I said, 'I am the Son of God'?"
     (John 10:35-36)

Reflection: The morning after a tense parish meeting, one
of the participants met with the pastor and apologized: "I'm
sorry I got into an argument at the committee meeting last
night, but I have a short temper. That's just the way I am."

But the wise and experienced pastor replied, "No, it's not.
You are who God made you to be, and God didn't make you
angry."

God did not "hardwire" us to be self-centered or angry or
narrow-minded; our need to be in control or our obsessive
focus on the "bottom line" is not our heaven-set default posi-
tion. We are not defined by the sum total of our failings and
limits.

In Christ, God shows us who he made us to be. In Jesus,
we see what it means to be created in the "image" of God.

This season of Lent is a mirror in which to see our lives, enabling us to realize what is of God and what is not. Lent calls us to a change of attitude and perspective that refuses to accept division and conflict as the price for doing business, that insists that the common good is more important than personal profit or gain, that the poor and struggling have places of honor at our tables.

In today's Gospel, Jesus replies to the Jews' growing resentment by citing Psalm 82, verse 6: "You are gods, children of the Most High, all of you." Considering ourselves "gods" may sound like the height of pretentiousness, but Jesus' point is that every human being possesses the grace that enables us to do the work of God: to love, to lift up, to heal, to bring back.

In the person of Jesus, St. Athanasius preached, "God became like us so that we might become like God." That's no exaggeration. As God entrusts the work of re-creation and reconciliation to his Son, the Son now entrusts that work to us. In baptism we are re-created in Christ; in baptism, we take on his work.

That's what God made us to be.

Meditation: In what way can you engage in some "God-like" work today?

Prayer: O God, you created us as your own and love as your sons and daughters. May your divinity in which we have been made and the spirit you have placed in our hearts enable us to do the work of reconciliation, justice, and peace begun by your Christ and now entrusted to us.

Rationalization 101

Readings: Ezek 37:21-28; John 11:45-56

Scripture:
   [Caiaphas] prophesied that Jesus was going to die for
      the nation,
   and not only for the nation,
   but also to gather into one the dispersed children of
      God. (John 11:51-52)

Reflection: Caiaphas is a master politician—as chief priest, he is responsible for the temple and the Sanhedrin, the ruling council of Jewish priests and Pharisees. He must walk a fine line between the interests of his own people and the power of their Roman masters occupying their homeland. He understands power and how to use it—and keep it. He is aware of the precariousness of his situation: he is high priest only by Roman consent—one misstep and he is finished.

   This Jesus is a complication that Caiaphas does not need. His talk of a kingdom of God may sound wonderful, but the notion of a "rival" kingdom makes the Romans very nervous and that's not good for anyone. And so the cynical Caiaphas sets in motion the plan to destroy Jesus. He rationalizes a quick course of action that "sounds good" to everyone: *Look, we have to protect ourselves. Rome is never going to tolerate this Jesus' claim to be a king. Better for him to die than for all of us to go down. So let's make sure we're on the right side of this.*

From Caiaphas' perspective, Jesus' death is the smart, politically expedient, pragmatic thing to do.

Like Caiaphas, we can rationalize our own actions to protect our interests. We know how to justify whatever we choose to do—or not do. Today's Gospel confronts us with the tension of balancing what we dream our lives to be and what they are; of staying secure on our "perches" in the face of so many forces that can knock us down; of our willingness to "crucify" reconciliation, justice and compassion on the cross of our own interests and ego.

The Gospel of Jesus' passion and death challenges us to confront the Caiaphas in all of us. Like Caiaphas, we can rationalize our own actions to protect our interests; we know how to justify whatever we do or refuse to do. But discipleship demands that we embrace our crosses as Jesus embraces his. The promise of the resurrection is fulfilled in our lives only when we make that Good Friday journey with Jesus.

Meditation: When have you rationalized some decision you made as necessary and right—when you knew it wasn't?

Prayer: Christ Jesus, may we walk with you to the kingdom of your Father, with courage to live your Gospel, with openness of heart to embrace your spirit of servanthood, with eagerness to bring your healing and peace to our families, communities, and world. May our faithfulness to your gospel compel us to seek your love in every relationship, your forgiveness in every crisis, your justice in every trial.

The Blessed Colt

Readings:
The Blessing and Procession of Palms: Mark 11:1-10
    or John 12:12-16
The Liturgy of the Word: Isa 50:4-7; Phil 2:6-11; Mark 14:1–15:47
    or Mark 15:1-39

Scripture:
[Jesus] sent two of his disciples and said to them,
"Go into the village opposite you,
and immediately on entering it,
you will find a colt tethered on which no one has ever
    sat.
Untie it and bring it here." (Mark 11:2)

Reflection: In his account of Jesus' Palm Sunday entry into Jerusalem, the evangelist Mark almost makes the colt—a young donkey—the center of the story. Mark recounts with surprising detail how the disciples found the colt as Jesus told them. Clearly, Jesus' riding the donkey into Jerusalem is no accident – Jesus intends that the colt play an important part in the Palm Sunday Gospel.

It was the custom for pilgrims to enter Jerusalem on foot. Only great kings and rulers would "ride" into the city, and usually on great steeds accompanied by a retinue of soldiers and servants. Jesus, the King of the new Israel, chooses to ride into the city not on a majestic stallion but on the back of a young beast of burden. By being led through the city on the back of a lowly beast of burden, Jesus comes as a king whose rule is not about being served but of *service*; his kingdom is not built on might but on *compassion*.

The colt mirrors how the prophet Zechariah foretold this scene five centuries before: "Exalt greatly, O daughter Zion! / Shout for joy, O daughter Jerusalem! / Behold: your king is coming to you, / a just savior is he, / Humble, and riding on a donkey, / on a colt, the foal of a donkey" (Zech 9:9, NABRE).

Let the little colt of today's Gospel guide you through the Holy Week ahead. Let him be the symbol of Christ's humility—a humility that is not self-loathing and self-diminishing but one that honors all men and women as children of God, a humility that enables us to love all humankind as brothers and sisters in Christ, a humility that rejoices in gratitude to God, the Author of all life.

Meditation: How might you follow the example of Jesus in "emptying" yourself for the sake of someone else?

Prayer: O Lord our Redeemer, may we not only remember your passion, death, and resurrection this Holy Week, but may we enter, heart and soul, into your "Passover" from death to life. Let the example of your humility guide our faltering steps as we struggle to follow you from Jerusalem to the Upper Room, from agony to trial, from crucifixion to burial. Help us to empty ourselves of our own hurts and wants in order to become vessels of your compassion for others.

Wasted

Readings: Isa 42:1-7; John 12:1-11

Scripture:
Mary took a liter of costly perfumed oil
   made from genuine aromatic nard
   and anointed the feet of Jesus and dried them with her
     hair;
   the house was filled with the fragrance of the oil.
    (John 12:3)

Reflection: It probably cost her everything she had—and yes, the money could have been used for more important things, things she and her own little family could have used, let alone how it might have helped the poor. It was an extravagant act that rocked her sister's dinner party. She might well have been overcome with gratitude to their guest for bringing their brother back from the grave. How do you thank someone who has given you back your dead brother?

Such extravagance infuriated the holder of the company's purse. This money could have been used for the poor, he protested—but it was the waste that angered him. Perfume to clean a guest's feet—please!

Mary's act is not a matter of extravagance and waste but one of gratitude and love. Her gift comes not from the extra she could spare but from her own need, her own poverty.

With a liter of ointment, she expresses a love she feels in the depths of her soul, a love that is beyond her ability to express in words she can articulate.

Judas' protestations sound reasonable, but he's not kidding anyone. Love and gratitude that are sincere and true transcend balance sheets and sound fiscal management.

This moment in John's gospel, which takes place less than a week before the evening of the Last Supper, calls us to approach the events of Holy Week by looking deeper than what we will simply see and hear. Throughout the Gospel of John, Jesus speaks of the reign of God as a matter of heart and spirit, a kingdom that cannot be measured by the standards of the world or the values of the marketplace. In the events of Holy Week, God speaks not in words and descriptions, but with bread and wine, a towel and basin, a human body broken and slain, an empty tomb—all expressing a love inexplicable and unfathomable.

Meditation: Is there some act of "extravagant" generosity that you can perform before the end of this week?

Prayer: Father, by his cross, your Son transformed our lives from despair to hope, from pain to wholeness, from sadness to joy, from death to life. Imitating his love and compassion and his humble attitude of selflessness for others, may we transform our heaviest crosses into opportunities for Easter transformation and new life. May we live our lives in the eternal hope that we are never "lost" but constantly found by your gracious providence.

March 31: Tuesday of Holy Week

Only Love Can Break Your Heart

Readings: Isa 49:1-6; John 13:21-33, 36-38

Scripture:
Peter said to [Jesus],
    "Master, why can I not follow you now?
    I will lay down my life for you."
Jesus answered, "Will you lay down your life for me?
Amen, amen I say to you, the cock will not crow
    before you deny me three times." (John 13:37-38)

Reflection: To say to another person "I love you" can be a dangerous thing. It is like free-falling into the abyss—or walking a high wire without a net.

To say "I love you" is the ultimate act of trust. You place yourself at the mercy of the other. Love is the gift of everything you have and are to another—there is no piece of yourself to hold on to, there is no turning back, there is no place to hide.

To say "I love you" is to place yourself at your most vulnerable.

To say "I love you" is to risk rejection and even ridicule.

To say "I love you" is to allow your heart to be broken.

To say "I love you" is to face possible betrayal.

We have all experienced the pain of being rejected or ridiculed. And, truth be told, we have all hurt those we love the most—the word "betray" is not too strong a word to describe how we have broken faith with them.

But that is exactly why those three words are so precious.

Today's Gospel reminds us of that important reality: that love means opening ourselves up to hurt. The Gospels of Holy Week illustrate the hope that such love is worth the risk, that the complete, total, and unconditional love that is of God will ultimately overcome any betrayal, bridge the deepest chasm, and heal the broken heart.

Easter hope is the grace to love fully and completely—not despite the risk but *because of* the risk. The promise of Easter is the blessed assurance that God, the Author of love, will vindicate our poor, faltering efforts to love, raising us up out of the ashes of love betrayed.

Meditation: What has made you hesitate to say "I love you" to someone? Have you ever regretted NOT saying it to someone?

Prayer: O God, help us to realize the implications of loving and understand the many ways our love deteriorates into betrayal and broken promises. May we prefer nothing to your love, and may we possess your courage and compassion to pay whatever price necessary to bring the promise of your resurrection into our desperate world.

Betrayal

Readings: Isa 50:4-9a; Matt 26:14-25

Scripture:
[The chief priests] paid [Judas] thirty pieces of silver,
   and from that time on he looked for an opportunity to
      hand him over. (Matt 26:15-16)

Reflection: *Betrayal* is British playwright Harold Pinter's story of a marriage that breaks apart. But Pinter tells the story backwards: the audience knows the ending at the outset. As the curtain opens, the couple has divorced and the former spouses begin to go their separate ways—then Pinter sets up a series of scenes portraying the acts of betrayal and mistrust that will lead to the end of the marriage.

The scenes between the husband and wife and the husband's best friend (whose own acts of "betrayal" contribute to the breakup) are painfully polite. The lines spoken are so innocuous, so meager, so couched that the audience must supply the missing words. From our own experience with relationships, from the pain we know of being betrayed by another, from the guilt of our own acts of betraying those we love, we "write" the play.

And we know the language of betrayal. We know how to avoid, how to remain aloof, how to stand back. We know how and when to fire that one word that will sting and hurt, we know how to stay in control, we know how to protect our own interests.

Today's Gospel recalls Judas' tragic act of betraying Jesus, supposedly for thirty pieces of silver. But many scholars have suggested that Judas betrays Jesus not for money but because of his disappointment that Jesus has not been the politically powerful Messiah he had hoped for. Or, to put it another way, Judas believes *he* was the one betrayed by Jesus.

We, too, use our own disappointment in others to justify our own acts of betrayal. The thirty pieces of silver we pocket are a pitifully small price for the hurt and destruction our betrayals can wreak.

Meditation: In what ways do you unintentionally or unconsciously "betray" others?

Prayer: Christ our Redeemer, open our eyes to see the many ways we betray you and one another; open our consciences to realize how afraid we are to do what is right and just. Help us to make the words of compassion and mercy we offer this Easter a dependable bond of trust and commitment between us and those we love.

April 2: Holy Thursday (Maundy Thursday)

Footwashers Among Us

Readings: Exod 12:1-8, 11-14; 1 Cor 11:23-26; John 13:1-15

Scripture:
"If I, therefore, the master and teacher, have washed your
   feet,
   you ought to wash one another's feet. . . .
   [A]s I have done for you, you should also do."
   (John 13:14-15)

Reflection: After a hard day at work, he comes home to his
beloved family. As he does every evening, he tucks a towel
around his waist and helps prepare the meal for the family,
bathe the children, wash the dishes—whatever needs to be
done. He will bend down to bandage a scraped knee, work
through the details of a school project, brush the tangles out
of his little girl's hair. The loving father with the towel tucked
around his waist imitates the love of Jesus, who washed the
feet of his disciples.

   Her years of college studies and hospital training all come
down to this: holding the hand of the terrified child during
the procedure, cleaning up the mess of an incontinent patient
and reassuring her despite her embarrassment, staying with
the sick man whose system cannot physically tolerate the
chemotherapy drugs. Nurses and caregivers understand the
meaning of tonight's Gospel, when Jesus washed the feet of
his disciples.

Footwashers abound in a parish—they put aside their own needs and wants to take on the low visibility tasks of preparing food for the poor, cleaning the sanctuary and shoveling the church walkways, taking on a weekly religious education class. In their service to the community, they discover the humble dignity of Jesus, who washed the feet of his disciples.

In the first act of his passion and death, Jesus leaves his final instruction to his new church: *Love one another as I have loved you: loved you enough to become one of you, loved you enough to give my life to you and for you, loved you enough to die for you, loved you enough to rise for you.* And Jesus memorializes his final teaching in bread, blessed and broken, and in a pitcher of water and towel.

To be footwashers in the spirit of Jesus is to see one another not as a demographic but as individual human beings with whom we share the dignity of being made in the image of God.

Meditation: In what ways can you "wash the feet" of someone you know, in the spirit of Jesus?

Prayer: Gracious Father, tonight we remember the beginning of Jesus' "Passover." As he washed the feet of his disciples, may we humbly and joyfully wash the feet of one another and allow others to wash our feet in a spirit of kindness and forgiveness. As we receive this night the bread and wine of the Eucharist, may we become Christ's body and blood for our broken, hurting world.

The Crosses We Bear

Readings: Isa 52:13–53:12; Heb 4:14-16; 5:7-9; John 18:1–19:42.

Scripture:
So they took Jesus, and, carrying the cross himself,
    he went out to what is called the Place of the Skull,
    in Hebrew, Golgotha.
There they crucified him, and with him two others,
    one on either side, with Jesus in the middle.
    (John 19:16-18)

Reflection: It may be the mountain of laundry you face every day or your child's tuition bill.

It could take the form of the textbooks you use to teach your students, the tools you wield at the construction site, the computer that produces the reports and graphics that keep your business humming along.

Yours may be the soup you make and serve at the local soup kitchen or the soccer ball you use to coach a team of excited six and seven-year-olds.

Some of the most beautiful ones are the ear that is always ready to listen to another's troubles, the shoulder always available for one to cry on, the smile that readily comforts, the heart that never fails to break with another.

Believe it or not, spouses are sometimes big ones for one another; good friends readily accept each other as one.

They are all *crosses.*

We tend to think of crosses as burdens, things—and people!—that demand so much energy and time from us. We see our sufferings and our brokenness as crosses that condemn us to living incomplete and unfulfilled lives of sadness and despair. Most days we would like to lay those crosses aside and never pick them up again.

But our real crosses—those God places on our shoulders and Christ bears with us—are sources of hope, of joy of discovery, of life, of resurrection—for both others and ourselves. They are not the limitations of our lives but the means to living our lives to the fullest, the vehicles for discovering the meaning and purpose of this journey God has set us on.

Today we remember the day Jesus, in a spirit of obedience and love, took up his cross. Clearly our crosses pale in the shadow of his. But as the wood of his cross becomes the tree of Easter life, our crosses, when taken up in his spirit of humility and compassion, can be no less than the first light of Easter dawn.

Meditation: What is your cross that enables you to bring resurrection into your life and into the lives of others?

Prayer: God of life, help us to realize your presence with us as we take up the crosses you place on our shoulders. By your grace, may we transform the crucifixions that take place around us into victories of the Easter promise. By your love, may we embrace Christ's spirit of humility to become servants to one another, so that we may share, as one family of humankind, the eternal life of the Risen One, Jesus the Christ.

The Angel's News This Easter

Readings: Gen 1:1–2:2 or 1:1, 26-31a; Gen 22:1-18 or 22:1-2, 9a, 10-13, 15-18; Exod 14:15–15:1; Isa 54:5-14; Isa 55:1-11; Bar 3:9-15, 32–4:4; Ezek 36:16-17a, 18-28; Rom 6:3-11; Mark 16:1-7

Scripture:
"Do not be amazed!
You seek Jesus of Nazareth, the crucified.
He has been raised; he is not here.
Behold the place where they laid him." (Mark 16:6)

Reflection: Every year we probably hear the Easter gospel a little differently. Where we are on our journeys to Jerusalem and Calvary affects what we hear and how we hear it. The words spoken by the angel resonate with different meanings as we move and change through life.

If you are celebrating the safe return of a lost son or daughter, the empty tomb is the assurance of God's protection during the darkest nights and along the most dangerous roads.

If you are mourning the loss of a spouse or child or dear friend, the angel's news may be the first light of hope to illuminate your broken heart: the promise that the Risen Christ has lovingly taken your loved one to the dwelling place of his Father.

If you've lost your job or if you and your family are struggling financially, the moving of the immovable rock is a sign of God's grace, enabling you to realize what is truly dear and important to you. In the sight of the stone rolled away, God extends his hand to lift you out of your despair and to help you realize the abilities and gifts you have to live your life with meaning and purpose.

Every Easter, a different piece or player of the Easter story speaks to our hearts and spirits, our fears and anxieties, depending on our particular circumstances. In this moment of our lives, in this time and place, God speaks to us in the words of the angel, in the site of the open grave, in the simple kindness of the myrrh bearers.

Whatever road you are traveling this Easter, whatever burial clothes you are struggling to free yourself from, whatever cross you are struggling to carry, may you find reason to hope—and may that hope free you to re-create your life in Easter joy, peace—and amazement.

Meditation: What particular element of the Easter Gospel speaks to you of hope and promise this year?

Prayer: Father of unfathomable compassion, re-create us in the love you loosed upon the world in the passion, death, and resurrection of your Son. Never let us lose hope that your love can transform the darkest nights of our lives into the glorious morning of Easter joy. May we be willing to let our own needs and wants die so that we might become something greater: sharers in the resurrection of your Son.

April 5: Easter Sunday

"While It Was Still Dark . . . "

Readings: Acts 10:34a, 37-43; Col 3:1-4 or 1 Cor 5:6b-8; John 20:1-9 or Mark 16:1-7

Scripture:
On the first day of the week,
   Mary of Magdala came to the tomb early in the
      morning,
   while it was still dark,
   and saw the stone removed from the tomb. (John 20:1)

Reflection: Easter begins in the dark. Always.

In all the accounts of the resurrection, Mary of Magdala (alone or with any number of her companions) comes to the tomb while it is still dark. She feels the predawn darkness around her and within her: a void of hopelessness, a crushing sense of loss, a grief that cannot be articulated in words.

Easter begins in the dark of night. If you have ever kept vigil at the bedside of a dying loved one or if you have ever been unable to sleep because of what was to come, Easter has dawned in your life. God has been with you through those long hours; God has embraced you in your isolation; God has come in the morning.

Easter begins in the dark earth. Easter is a seed planted in the new spring soil that struggles through the winter hardness to blossom. If you've ever struggled to remake your life in the wake of loss, hurt, or devastation, Easter has dawned in your life. Easter reveals that death is not the final ending but the passage to the God who first breathed life into you.

Easter begins in ashes. If you've ever been swallowed up in hopelessness or fear or if you've ever been paralyzed by hurt or ill-treatment, Easter has dawned in your life. No matter how hard we fall, no matter how broken we are, no matter how deep the chasm into which we've fallen, Easter is the Risen One walking in your midst in the compassion of loved ones, the support of friends, the dedication of saints.

Easter begins in the darkness of night, in the seeming finality of earth, in the hopelessness of ashes.

But Easter moves beyond those states.

Easter is the eternal morning after the darkest, stormiest night. Easter is the stubborn hope of a God who re-creates our world until his dream of a humanity bound in his love is realized. Easter is the risen Christ in our midst, enabling us to mend our broken lives in his compassion and peace.

The dark night has ended. Morning has broken. *Alleluia!*

Meditation: In what darkness does this Easter begin for you this year? What hope or change illuminates that darkness?

Prayer: Father, this day we celebrate the empty tomb of your Son—your ultimate promise of hope, of life, of love for humanity. May the joy of this Easter morning give us the grace and courage to abandon the tombs we create for ourselves and welcome the resurrection into our lives; to renew and re-create our world in the light of the Risen One; to proclaim in every moment of our lives the Gospel of the Easter Christ.

References

February 20: Friday after Ash Wednesday
Rabbi Joseph Telushkin, *The Book of Jewish Values: A Day-by-Day Guide to Ethical Living* (New York: Bell Tower, 2000), 106.

February 23: Monday of the First Week of Lent
Nikos Kazantzakis, *The Greek Passion* (New York: Simon & Schuster, 1954), 229–30.

February 24: Tuesday of the First Week of Lent
Rachel Naomi Remen, *My Grandfather's Blessings: Stories of Strength, Refuge, and Belonging* (New York: Riverhead, 2000), 216–17.

February 26: Thursday of the First Week of Lent
Father Nonomen, "A Hole in the Basket: With Sunday Collections, You Get What You Give," *Commonweal*, February 7, 2014.

February 28: Saturday of the First Week of Lent
Kate Braestrup, *Marriage and Other Acts of Charity: A Memoir* (New York: Little, Brown, 2010), 61–62.

March 4: Wednesday of the Second Week of Lent
Donald L. Anderson, "Caring Really Counts—and Costs," *Princeton Seminary Bulletin* 8, no. 1 (February 1987).

March 6: Friday of the Second Week of Lent
Eric Hague, *In the Shadow of Nine Dragons* (London: The Highway Press, 1958), 106–8.

March 9: Monday of the Third Week of Lent
Margaret Silf, "The Power of One," *America*, July 6–13, 2009.

March 13: Friday of the Third Week of Lent
Anne Lamott, *Bird by Bird: Some Instructions on Writing and Life* (New York: Pantheon, 1994), 205.

March 15: Fourth Sunday of Lent
Lauren F. Winner, *Still: Notes on a Mid-Faith Crisis* (New York: HarperOne, 2012), xiii–xiv.

March 18: Wednesday of the Fourth Week of Lent
Nathaniel Hawthorne, "The Minister's Black Veil," *Hawthorne's Short Stories* (New York: Vintage Classics, 1946), 22–23.

March 26: Thursday of the Fifth Week of Lent
Alfonso Cuarón (director) and Alonso Cuarón and Jonas Cuarón (screenwriters), *Gravity* (Warner Bros. Pictures, 2013).

March 27: Friday of the Fifth Week of Lent
M. Craig Barnes, *The Pastor as Minor Poet: Texts and Subtexts in the Ministerial Life* (Grand Rapids, MI: Wm B. Eerdmans, 2008), 94.